First Biographies

Marie Curie

by Lola M. Schaefer and Wyatt Schaefer

Consulting Editor: Gail Saunders-Smith, PhD
Consultant: Spencer R. Weart, Director
Center for the History of Physics
American Institute of Physics
College Park, Maryland

Capstone
press
Mankato, Minnesota

Pebble Books are published by Capstone Press
151 Good Counsel Drive, P.O. Box 669, Mankato, Minnesota 56002
www.capstonepress.com

1 2 3 4 5 6 09 08 07 06 05 04

Library of Congress Cataloging-in-Publication Data
Schaefer, Lola M., 1950–
 Marie Curie / by Lola M. Schaefer and Wyatt Schaefer.
 p. cm.—(First biographies)
 Includes bibliographical references and index.
 ISBN 0-7368-2084-1 (hardcover)
 1. Curie, Marie, 1867–1934—Juvenile literature. 2. Chemists—Poland—
Biography—Juvenile literature. [1. Curie, Marie, 1867–1934. 2. Chemists.
3. Women—Biography.] I. Schaefer, Wyatt S., 1978- II. Title. III. Series: First
biographies (Mankato, Minn.)
QD22.C8S32 2005
540'.92—dc22   2003025607

Summary: Simple text and photographs present the life of Marie Curie, the scientist
who discovered radium.

Note to Parents and Teachers

The First Biographies series supports national history standards
for units on people and culture. This book describes and illustrates
the life of Marie Curie. The photographs support early readers in
understanding the text. This book also introduces early readers
to subject-specific vocabulary words, which are defined in the
Glossary. Early readers may need assistance to read some words
and to use the Table of Contents, Glossary, Read More, Internet
Sites, and Index/Word List sections of the book.

Table of Contents

Time Line

● 1867
born

4

Young Marie

Marie Curie was a famous scientist. She was born in Poland in 1867. She had three sisters and one brother.

Marie (left) with her sister Bronya in 1886

Time Line

1867
born

1891
moves to
Paris

Marie moved to Paris, France, in 1891. She studied math and physics. Marie was the best student in her class.

Marie in Paris in 1891

Time Line

1867
born

1891
moves to
Paris

1895
marries
Pierre Curie

Marie and Pierre

In 1895, Marie married Pierre Curie. They worked together in a science lab in Paris.

Pierre and Marie in 1895

Time Line

1867
born

1891
moves to
Paris

1895
marries
Pierre Curie

Marie and Pierre had two daughters. Irene was born in 1897. Eve was born in 1904.

Irene (left), Marie, and Eve (on Marie's lap) in 1905

Time Line

1867	1891	1895	1898
born	moves to Paris	marries Pierre Curie	discovers radium

Marie taught classes in Paris. She also did science experiments. In 1898, Marie and Pierre discovered radium. Radium is a white element.

◀ Marie in her lab

Time Line

1867
born

1891
moves to
Paris

1895
marries
Pierre Curie

1898
discovers
radium

Radium became important in science. Doctors treated cancer with radium. In 1903, Marie and Pierre won the Nobel Prize in physics for their work with radium.

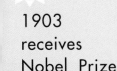

Marie and Pierre in their lab around 1903

1903
receives
Nobel Prize

Time Line

1867
born

1891
moves to
Paris

1895
marries
Pierre Curie

1898
discovers
radium

Famous Scientist

Pierre died in 1906. Marie kept working in the lab. In 1911, she won the Nobel Prize in chemistry. She was the first person to win two Nobel Prizes.

 Marie in her lab around 1913

1903
receives
Nobel Prize

1911
receives second
Nobel Prize

Time Line

1867
born

1891
moves to
Paris

1895
marries
Pierre Curie

1898
discovers
radium

Marie founded the Radium Institute in 1914. Scientists there studied ways to use radium.

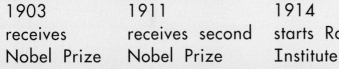

◀ the Radium Institute in Paris around 1955

1903
receives
Nobel Prize

1911
receives second
Nobel Prize

1914
starts Radium
Institute

Time Line

```
    1867        1891         1895          1898
    born        moves to     marries       discovers
                Paris        Pierre Curie  radium
```

Marie died in 1934. Today, scientists at the Radium Institute continue her work. People remember Marie as a great scientist.

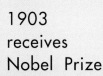 Marie around 1930

1903
receives
Nobel Prize

1911
receives second
Nobel Prize

1914
starts Radium
Institute

1934
dies

Glossary

cancer—a disease in which unhealthy cells in the body grow quickly and destroy healthy body parts

chemistry—the scientific study of substances and their composition

element—a basic substance in chemistry that cannot be split into simpler substances

experiment—a scientific test to find out how something works

Nobel Prize—an award given to a person who makes a great contribution to the world; Marie Curie won one Nobel Prize for physics and one for chemistry.

physics—the science that deals with matter and energy; physics includes the study of light, heat, sound, electricity, motion, and force.

radium—a white radioactive metal element; radium was once used to treat cancer; radium can be harmful when not used correctly.

scientist—a person who studies science

Read More

Gogerly, Liz. *Marie Curie.* Scientists Who Made History. Austin, Texas: Raintree Steck-Vaughn, 2001.

Rau, Dana Meachen. *Marie Curie.* Early Biographies. Minneapolis: Compass Point Books, 2001.

Santella, Andrew. *Marie Curie.* Trailblazers of the Modern World. Milwaukee: World Almanac Library, 2001.

Internet Sites

FactHound offers a safe, fun way to find Internet sites related to this book. All of the sites on FactHound have been researched by our staff.

Here's how:

1. Visit *www.facthound.com*

2. Type in this special code **0736820841** for age-appropriate sites. Or enter a search word related to this book for a more general search.

3. Click on the **Fetch It** button.

FactHound will fetch the best sites for you!

Index/Word List

Word Count: 182
Early-Intervention Level: 19

Editorial Credits
Martha E. H. Rustad, editor; Heather Kindseth, cover designer and illustrator;
   Enoch Peterson, production designer; Kelly Garvin, photo researcher; Karen Hieb,
   product planning editor

Photo Credits
Corbis/Bettmann, 4, 10, 16
Getty Images/Hulton Archive, cover, 1, 6, 8, 12, 14, 18, 20